SATOMI ICHIKAWA

A Child's Book of Seasons

c. 2

Parents' Magazine Press • New York

Copyright © 1975 by Satomi Ichikawa
All rights reserved
Printed in the United States of America
Published 1975 by William Heinemann Ltd., London
Published 1976 by Parents' Magazine Press

Library of Congress Cataloging in Publication Data
Ichikawa, Satomi.
    A child's book of seasons.
    SUMMARY: Pictures and text lovingly portray activities of
children throughout the year.
    1. Seasons — Juvenile poetry. [1. Seasons — Poetry]
I. Title.
PZ8.3.I25   811   74-31047
ISBN 0-8193-0795-5   ISBN 0-8193-0796-3 lib. bdg.

A CHILD'S BOOK OF SEASONS

Please take a look inside this book to see what children do
In snow and sunshine, wind and rain, the changing seasons through.

In the cold and wintry sun
Round the schoolyard children run.

They jump and skip and play at ball
And pushmepullyou by the wall.

Pitter, patter, here's the rain!
Children hurry home again

To stay indoors while long hours pass
And raindrops scurry down the glass.

They play doctor and soldier and rider of grace
And elegant ladies in lipstick and lace.

Out comes the sun, and all rush to the sill
To see the bright rainbow bend over the hill.

Oh, to peep over a garden wall,
Then to come in and play,

Next to share warm flower-petal jam
At the end of a bright June day.

Leaves rustle softly and whisper and sway—
Can you see in the boughs who is hidden away?

Green is the grass, and green the deep sea,
But nothing's so green as the world of a tree.

In the heat of midsummer, there's all day to play.
Children sprinkle each other and ride through the spray.

They pedal down a winding road that leads beyond the town
And stop to see the grazing cows, spotted black or brown.

Oooh! How the cool stream tickles hot toes
As over the pebbles it swiftly flows.

Someone is taking a nap in the shade
Dreaming of snack time and iced lemonade.

Two, four, six, eight,
Trotting through an open gate.

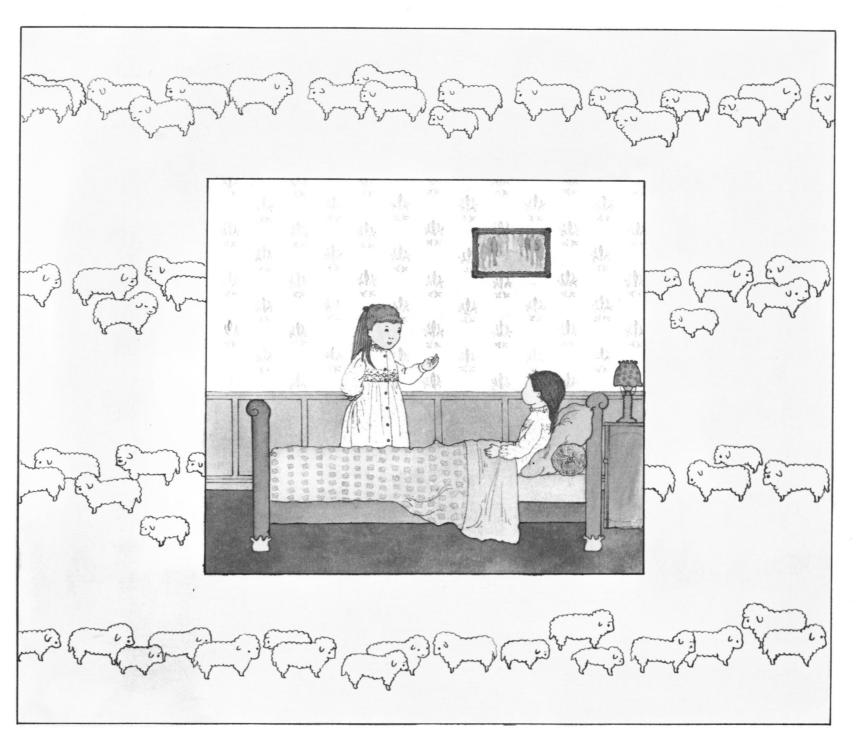

(Try to count those silly sheep
And soon you'll find you're fast asleep.)

Out in the farmyard, children scatter the feed.
Hungry chicks and geese will snatch up all they need.

The mowing of hayfields and clover is done,
And barn swallows flock in the setting sun.

Along the roadside berries grow—juicy, ripe, and red.
Children drop them into baskets (or open mouths instead).

Carrots, corn, and cauliflower are piled high on the cart,
But the stubborn little donkey just won't make a start.

In autumn, horse chestnuts grow fat on the tree.
Shaking and tapping set most of them free.

Leaves turn saffron, russet, brown—
Children catch them sailing down.

Soft in winter falls the snow
Like feathers on the ground below.

Wrapped up warmly children play
With snow and snowmen through the day.

In silvery woods the trees stand tall and still
As children trudge homeward beneath the white hill.

Candles and stars give a glimmering light:
Each child hangs a stocking, then whispers "Goodnight."

Satomi Ichikawa is a young
Japanese artist living in Paris.
Largely self-taught, she turned
to children's book illustration
after discovering the work of
the turn-of-the-century French
master illustrator, Maurice
Boutet de Monvel.